Shape Soul

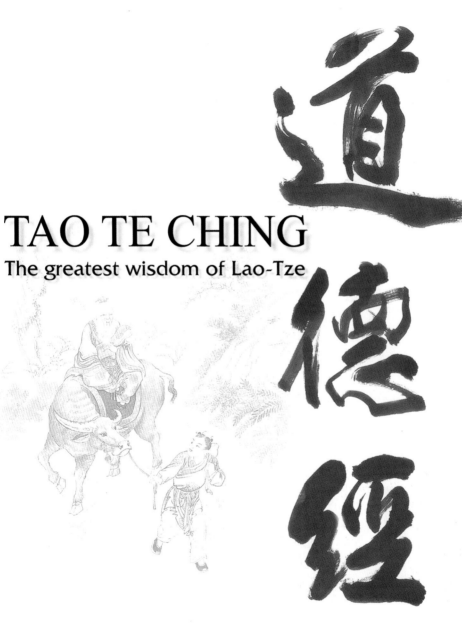

# TAO TE CHING

## The greatest wisdom of Lao-Tze

      ISBN
      E-mail: iktfoa@earthlink.net

Translated by:Theresa Sun
Editing consultant:Frank Shih
Artistic work by:Artist Shuang Kwan Wang
Digital Art Edited by:Shu-Mei Huang
English proofread by:Theresa Sun
Chinese proofread by: Master Chin Lung Lin
                Master Geng Sheng Zhao

This book is dedicated to those who would like to be
enlightened by the

Great Wisdom of Universal Truth

And find the spiritual path of unity with the
Oneness towards

Eternal freedom and peace

The greatest wisdom of Lao-Tze

道德經
TAO TE CHING

道本一體
理無二致

張培成題

# Foreword

The book of 'Tao Te Ching' by Lao-Tze has been around for more than 2,500 years. It was in the late Epoch of Warring States in China that this classic was completed and wide-spreaded. 'Tao Te Ching' has profoundly influenced the Chinese culture, and hence Chuang Tze praised Lao Tze as the ancient well-learned Immortal. He also indicated that the essence of TAO is to cultivate oneself and nurture the true nature.

This classic book involves all aspects from philosophy, ethics, politics to military science etc., and implies the idea of 'Return to the original truth and simplicity'. The essence of TAO of Lao-Tze is the nature law of the universe and the 'WAY of Life'. IT is the ultimate union of Nature and men, the transformation of ancient to present, the way to peace on earth, the universal truth of mysticism of the immortal. It is 'THE WAY' for earthly man to cultivate one's true nature to return to the pure 'Oneness'.

Generally speaking, from universe to mankind, from ancient to modern, TAO embraces all and everything. IT can be worldly, secluded or transcendent.

TAO is the mystics of the mystics, and IT is the origin of all *science. Therefore, regardless of western or orient, ancient or modern,' TAO TE CHING' is altogether a classic book of profound influence.*

*TAO is the nature's law and we human are a part of nature. We and the nature are under the regulation of this Great TAO. If mankind can let go of their selfish desire, act a natural act, and act freely, then we are sure to unite with TAO as one; TAO is me, and I am TAO.*

*As a fact, TAO does not depart from man. It is man who depart from TAO. Men often depend on the limited knowledge they have acquired and tried to reform, conquer and enslave the nature.*

*In fact, the more modernized human are, although accumulated more science and high technology, their spiritual world is more and more distressed. Hence high technology and materialism cannot bring peace to one's mind and spirit, rather that the cause of isolating oneself from the Nature TAO, the Great TAO. Thus "Man departs from TAO".*

Great TAO lies not in words and knowledge. The proverb says: "Water that sounds is not real, emptiness comes after a flying bird, shadow is but an illusion, dream is vain and unreal". Let go of all false appearances and wild fantasy, act naturally without desire and act with freedom, Great TAO thus is present.

The book of "TAO TE CHING" by Lao-Tze is the unique cultural treasure of China and the world. Theresa Sun has devoted one year of her endeavor to interpretate and translate this classic book of wisdom.

She has truly contributed to the dissemination of the traditional culture of wisdom and virtue. This is a great value of the millennium and important inspiration to future education.

施慶星

Chairman of I-kuan TAO
Foundation at Taiwan

# PREFACE

The translation of this edition of TAO TE CHING ( The Greatest Wisdom ) from Chinese into English was first inspired by my experience in an English study group of " TAO TE CHING " at I-Kuan Tao Foundation  in Fremont, California. I was deeply touched by the ingenious wisdom of Lao Tze and his wonderful spirit in pursuing the natural truth of life while reading through the Chinese version of  " TAO TE CHING ".

However, when it comes to the English study group of " TAO TE CHING ", although I had six different editions of English translations at hand and also researched through more than ten different English translation versions, I was surprised to find that those translations were based on literal meaning which is mainly from the scholastic point of views while some other translations were overly religious that seemed to overlook the true essence and spirit of Lao Tze. Therefore with the limited English translations, it was ambiguous and confusing for the English "TAO TE CHING" study group to comprehend the spirit and great wisdom of Lao-Tze in a consistent manner.

At this point, I was encouraged by honorable Master Wu to start the mission of translating the English "TAO TE CHING".

I am honored and very thankful to have this opportunity to receive this great task. However, this is a difficult mission to try to understand and translate Lao-Tze's wondrous work of the Integral Truth and Great Wisdom. The faith and courage that drives me forward to complete this honorable task comes from the inner spirit and true nature of the ONENESS that constantly guides and inspires me to sense with my heart all the wonders that are around. ( Those who are interested in more details, please E-mail to taoteching@prodigy.net or write to 3195 Calaveras road, Milpitas, CA 95035 ).

Our goal is to present Lao Tze's "TAO TE CHING" as original and as complete as possible. Our focus is to reveal his teachings that are both rational and miraculous which appear to be like a cup of clear and flavorless water, yet their subtle profundity is immeasurable. They are the expression of utmost simplicity and purest wisdom. They enable people at all levels of development to be inspired by this great wisdom, just as pure water refreshes and supports all forms of life.

The essence of Lao-Tze's teaching is in the form of " Mind Teaching" which is beyond and transcends all thoughts, words, and knowledge. It is our wish to provide with this classics of "TAO TE CHING" a guidance towards the perfect harmony of ONE-NESS to unite all beings and the universe.

Ever since I was a little girl, I always felt like I was a child of the nature. Being with all the natural lives and things around me, I feel free and complete. The mystic source and mystics of life has always fascinated me. So this inner spirit has guided me through childhood, then medical school from Taiwan University, Master of Clinical Immunology from Hahnemann University, Philadelphia, cancer research in Chiron corporation, California, and finally to my destiny, the spiritual health of medicine.

I was enlightened and initiated with TAO in 1987 and has pursued my spiritual path ever since. As a TAO cultivator, it is my mission to spread the Universal Truth of TAO and the great wisdom of Lao-Tze through three levels of existence, that is The Physical, The Mind, and The Spirit.

I regard this mission of translation as sacred and honorable, although personally I am lowly and humble. It is my mission to fulfill this great task to provide an opportunity for easier learning and enlightenment for those who are in search of the

*Universal Truth, True Freedom and Happiness.*

*This challenging and difficult work of translation is an accomplishment made possible by the inspiration and guidance from the honorable masters, friends and all heart-felt life energy around me. They are the real authors that are most precious in this complete work of translation. This edition of English translation of " TAO TE CHING " ( The Greatest Wisdom ) is meant to elucidate the core essence of TAO and the Three Treasures that runs consistently through the book. We hope that the message of the Universal Truth of Lao- Tze will be received by those who are in search of the meaning of life and will help them to be enlightened with TAO.*

*As for those who have attained TAO and are on their WAY to cultivate themselves, we wish that this book will further strengthen their faith of understanding the Three Treasures of life and provide a guidance in spiritual growth for those who are still seeking for the enlightenment of life.*

# Acknowledgements

*THANK YOU TO MY FAMILY, especially my husband, Frank Shih for his continuous loving support and helpful suggestions to make this honorable mission possible. Also I want to express my heartfelt thanks to my five year-old daughter, Venus Shih for inspiring me with the miracles of life and has since transformed my life.*

*I am grateful to honorable Master Jin Mu Chen in guiding me with the enlightenment of the great wisdom of Lao-Tze to make possible this translation work to go beyond the literal translation and transcend into the mind and spirit of the teaching of Lao-Tze.*

*I also want to express special thanks to honorable Master Chin Lung Lin for his generous support and encouragement as a mentor. Also with my sincere thanks towards honorable Masters Zhong Xiong Wu and Geng Sheng Zhao. It is also my pleasure to give thanks to all the enthusiastic and passionate assistance and support from Master Gin Li Tsai, Fung Yui Wu, and Yung Tzai Jeng.*

*My gratitude also goes toward the editing group of*

CHI CHU MORAL CULTURE AND EDUCATION FOUNDATION IN TAIWAN including Master Fong Ming Pan, Ms. Hwei Ming Tai and Master Wen Ching Liu for their important and helpful assistance.

Most of all, thanks to you readers for sharing this inspiring Truth and Wisdom of the great ancient, Lao-Tze. May your life be filled with the joy of true freedom, peace and harmony.

And finally thank you the Great ONENESS for guiding all mankind with the light of True Nature.

A special note of appreciation towards most honorable and respectful artist, Shuang Kuan Wang for his contribution of the vivid presentation of this grand work of Lao-Tze. And also with special thanks towards Mr. Wang's artistic family, his wife Lih-Ru Cheng, his son Woei-Ming Wang, and his daughter-in-law Sheau Yi Wang for their enthusiastic particpation.

The respectful artist, Shuang Kuan Wang has devoted all his life into the world of art since he was a child, and had en-dured tremendous hardships in his early life as an artist. He is

now an acknowledged and well respected artist in the area of portrait painting. He has won countless awards in his artistic life including the award of the 34th president Eisenhower of the United States of America when he was eighteen years of age.

TAO TE CHING

# INTRODUCTION

*The book of "TAO TE CHING" by Lao-Tze is an ancient classic of the great wisdom of all mankind. It is greatly valued and honored because of its simplicity and yet profound wisdom of Truth. It was known that "TAO TE CHING" was originally written on slips of bamboos. And since the original characters were in Chinese, which are in fact pictograms and images of the nature and universe, therefore "TAO TE CHING" can also be regarded as a book of secret coding of the great universe and of the essence of life.*

*Although "TAO TE CHING" is a Chinese classic, it has fascinated people all over the world and has been frequently translated into various languages world wide.*

*"TAO TE CHING" is the most important document in Chinese culture and possibly in mankind's history to elucidate the correlation of the perfect union of human and Nature.*

# THE LIFE OF LAO-TZE

*It is important to know some background of the life of Lao-Tze to help us understand his teachings.*

*According to the ancient documents, Lao-Tze was regarded as a divine spiritual being. The legend states that when he was born he was already eighty-one years old, his hair was white as snow yet his face is innocent as an infant and hence got his name Lao-Tze meaning in English " The Old Child ". It is inspiring to think that it would take Lao-Tze eighty-one years to stay in his mother's womb to bear the fruit of wisdom.*

*It was recorded in Shih chi ( Records of the Historian, 63: 1a-3b ) that Lao-Tze ( the old master ) held the official title " keeper of archives " in the imperial court of the Chou Dynasty ( 1122-249 B.C. ). It was said that his birth place was Ku County of Chu, a powerful state existing from 740-330 B.C., which is now called Deer County in Hunan Province. The exact location where he was born is now the District of Chiu Ren where there is a temple commemorating Lao-Tze's spiritual achievement. Lao-Tze was recognized by the ancient achieved ones as the most highly*

achieved being. Lao-Tze's special achievement is not something that can be discussed as a knowledge, or some kind of astrology chart. It is a unique internal spiritual essence that is an integral part of the nature itself.

It was recorded that Confucius ( 551- 479 B.C. ) known as the greatest sage and teacher of Chinese history went to visit Lao-Tze several times and once commented to his student, " I know birds can fly, fish can swim, and animals can run. However, even the fastest animal can be trapped by people. A fast swimming fish can be caught in a net, and a fast flying bird can be entrapped. However a dragon is in the cloud above Heaven, it is unpredictable, and of immeasurable profundity. Today I have met Lao-Tze, and I believe he is a dragon." According to this reference, it can be perceived that Lao-Tze is a mystical being of utmost wisdom and integral truth that is beyond description and hence the exact documentation of the birth and death of Lao-Tze is not verifiable.

Lao-Tze lived in the Spring and Autumn, Warring States Era of the Chou dynasty which is in a time of great turmoil and spiritual disintegration. Thus he saw the time had come for him to leave the society of confusion and contention. So he rode westward on the back of a water buffalo to live a life in harmony with nature. When he came to the Han Gu pass at the border of China, he was requested by the official of the pass to write down the essence of his wisdom as a guidance for future generation. And hence resulted in this classic book of "TAO TE CHING". This book consists of a little more than five thousand words and is divided into eighty-one chapters which became available to all of us around 2,500 years ago. This classic is of great value to all people from the past to the future generations.

It is our hope that this book of English translation of "TAO TE CHING" can serve as a helpful reference and guidance in individual growth of the spirit and the mind as well as the physical well-being. The following three levels are further elucidation of the Universal Truth and the Universal Way of the Great TAO :

## I. TAO

Truth About Oneself

Truth About Oneness

Originally, TAO TE CHING was not divided into chapters. It

*was Hu San Gong ( the Old Gentleman of the River ) who divided the book into two parts with eighty-one chapters:*

*The first part which elucidates TAO, was thirty-seven chapters long, and the second part which elucidates TE, was forty-four chapters long.*

*TAO is the center of this classic book and is consistently elaborated through the chapters. Lao-Tze revealed TAO as the profound mystery that is the origin of the universe and the core essence of nature. From TAO, all beings came alive ( chapter one ). Although IT is regarded as void and intangible ( chapter fourteen ), IT is the true essence of all life form. Therefore TAO is in fact the empty void that is filled with the essence of life energy, IT is void yet full of vitality. This is the important principle that Lao-Tze tries to emphasize and enlighten we worldly people with the wish to awaken us to our true nature within. And this enlightenment is the mystic gate to the Three Treasures of life ( those who are interested in more details, please E-mail to taoteching@prodigy. net or write to 3195 Calaveras road, Milpitas, CA, USA ).*

*Since Lao-Tze lived in a time of confusion and disorder, his great work of "TAO TE CHING" was written during that era, we can relate the time period that Lao-Tze lived to the world today which is in a similar situation of confusion and disorder that is resulted from the overly developed materialized society. Therefore, it is clear that Lao-Tze's teaching of enlightenment is well suited for the past and the future and of all times. It is his wish to guide people to the original "ONENESS" that is shared by all differences, with the hope to unite all beings with the universe as a complete harmony.*

## II . TE
### Towards Eternity

*This level of enlightenment extends from the true essence of life and universe. Lao-Tze further elucidates his great wisdom of teaching by guiding the earthly people to realize that TE is the constant being originated from the constant void which enables one to see the outward manifestations of the great TAO of nature.*

*Hence, it is implied that from the smallness of personal life to the greatness of universal life, all should follow the natural path of TE with the sound foundation of the true essence. This is the key to reach the perfect union of Nature and men. What is TE? Lao-Tze said, " The mysterious nature creates and nurtures all things without the desire to possess them.*

*IT performs with all efforts without claiming for credit.*

*IT flourishes all beings without the intention to take control of. Such is the Mystic TE. " ( chapter ten )*

*By cultivating oneself with "Mystic TE", one's inner virtue is in accordance with the true nature and hence is filled with the essence of life and thus attain the perfect harmony of one's physical being, mind and spirit.*

## III. CHING

**Ching in English meaning " The WAY of Life ".**

*Ching is the WAY of life of Lao-Tze. It is also his wish to inspire all the earthly people to live a life of his or her own book of "TAO TE CHING". It is essential for each of us to be enlightened and initiated with TAO to recover our true nature ( those who are* interested , please E-mail to taoteching@prodigy.net or write to 3195 Calaveras road, Milpitas, CA95035, USA ).

In this twenty-first century of millennium, mankind has developed into an extravagant life style of luxurious materialized living. This extreme development of high technology and artificial intelligence has caused a negative impact on mankind's spiritual well-being. It is more than ever that the computerized new age of people are greatly thirsty of the enrichment of their spiritual growth to attain the harmony of one's overall health.

Therefore, with the development of the advance materialistic civilization by the westerners, it is also them who are awaken and are aware of the need to restore the deficiency in mankind's spiritual civilization. It is then that the ancient Chinese traditional culture such as Confucianism of morality and Lao-Tze's "TAO TE CHING" of Universal Truth had been uncovered and was highly honored and regarded as a  hope to reform and correct the world of chaos and disintegration.

This classic book of Lao-Tze is to inspire us to return to the common root of all beings and all things. Most importantly the "Nature WAY" to achieve this goal is to cherish and lead a simple life ( chapter eighty ).

Finally, Lao-Tze set the ideal for a perfect harmonious and peaceful world which is definitely not a world of secluded hermits. But rather that he hoped for a world that honors "TAO", cultivates with "TE" , and follows the "Nature WAY". This profound yet simple essence of "TAO TE CHING" is the great wisdom of Lao-Tze.

The greatest wisdom of Lao-Tze

道德經

TAO TE CHING

25

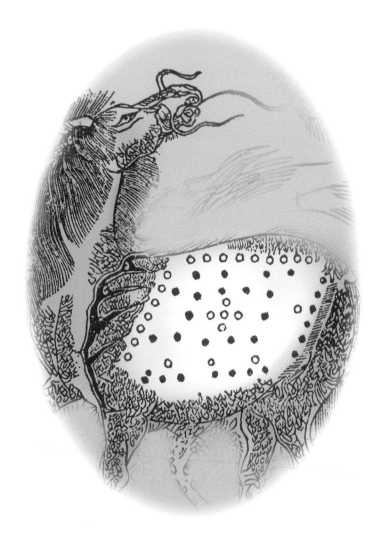

# 觀妙章 第一

道可道，非常道；名可名，非常名。

無，名天地之始；有，名萬物之母。

故常無，欲以觀其妙；常有，欲以觀其徼。

此兩者，同出而異名，同謂之玄，

玄之又玄，眾妙之門。

## CHAPTER ONE

Tao ( The Way ) that can be spoken of is not the Constant Tao;

The name that can be named is not a Constant Name.

Nameless, is the origin of Heaven and Earth;

The named is the Mother of all things.

Thus, the constant void enables one to observe the true essence.

The constant being enables one to see the outward manifestations.

These two come paired from the same origin.

But when the essence is manifested,

IT has a different name.

This same origin is called " The Profound Mystery ".

As profound the mystery as IT can be,

IT is the GATE to the essence of all life.

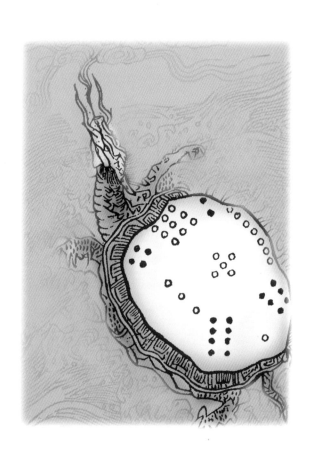

## 觀徼章　第二

天下皆知美之爲美，斯惡已。皆知善之爲善，斯不善已。
故有無相生，難易相成，長短相形，高下相傾，音聲相和，
前後相隨。是以聖人處無爲之事，行不言之敎。萬物作焉而不辭。
生而不有，爲而不恃，功成而弗居。夫唯弗居，是以不去。

# CHAPTER TWO

As soon as beauty is known by the world as beautiful, it becomes ugly.
As soon as virtue is being known as something good, it becomes evil.
Therefore being and non-being give birth to each other.

Difficult and easy accomplish each other.
Long and short form each other.
High and low distinguish each other.
Sound and tone harmonize each other.
Before and after follow each other as a sequence.

Realizing this, the saint performs effortlessly according to the
    natural WAY without personal desire, and practices the
    wordless teaching thru one's deeds.

The saint inspires the vitality of all lives, without
    holding back.
He nurtures all beings with no wish to take possession of.
He devotes all his energy but has no intention to hold on to the merit.
When success is achieved, he seeks no recognition.
Because he does not claim for the credit, hence shall not lose it.

# 安民章 第三

不尙賢，使民不爭；不貴難得之貨，使民不爲盜；
不見可欲，使民心不亂。
是以聖人之治：虛其心，實其腹；弱其志，強其骨。
常使民無知、無欲。使夫智者不敢爲也，爲無爲，則無不治。

## CHAPTER　THREE

By not adoring the worthy, people will not fall into dispute.
By not valuing the hard to get objects, people will not become
    robbers.
By not seeing the desires of lust, one's heart will not be confused.

Therefore the governing of the saint is to empty one's mind,
    substantiate one's virtue, weaken one's worldly ambition and
    strengthen one's essence.
He lets the people to be innocent of worldly knowledge and desire.
    And keeps the clever ones from making trouble with their wits.

Act naturally without desire, then everything will be accomplished
    in its natural order.

# 不盈章 第四

道沖而用之，或不盈。淵兮似萬物之宗。
挫其銳，解其紛，和其光，同其塵。
湛兮似或存。吾不知誰之子，象帝之先。

## CHAPTER　FOUR

TAO ( The Way ) can be infused into the nature and put to use
　　without being exhausted.
IT is so deep and subtle like an abyss that is the origin of all things.

IT is complete and perfect as a wholeness that can
　　Round off sharp edges;
　　Resolve confusion;
　　Harmonize with the glory;
　　Act in unity with the lowliness.

TAO is so profound and yet invisible, IT exists in everywhere
　　and anywhere.
I do not know whose Son IT is, IT existed before heaven and earth.

# 守中章　第五

天地不仁，以萬物爲芻狗，聖人不仁，以百姓爲芻狗，
天地之間，其猶橐籥乎！虛而不屈，動而愈出。
多言數窮，不如守中。

## CHAPTER FIVE

Nature nurtures all things with the wholeness of complete virtue.
　　It shows the greatest and perfect kindness by giving life to let all
　　things grow and accomplish them with the hastening of harvest.

Therefore, according to ancient custom, nature may seem unkind
　　to regard all beings as a traditional straw dog for sacrifice.
And likewise with a saint, he may seem unkind to regard people
　　as a traditional straw dog for sacrifice.

The space between heaven and earth is like the bellows,
　　it appears empty yet it gives a supply that never fails;
　　The more it moves, the more it brings forth.

Many words lead to exhaustion.
　　It is better to center on the true essence within.

The greatest wisdom of Lao-Tze

道德經
TAO TE CHING

# 谷神章　第六

谷神不死，是謂玄牝。
玄牝之門，是謂天地根。
綿綿若存，用之不勤。

## CHAPTER SIX

Spirit of the valley is immortal.

IT is called the mystic nature.

The gate of the mystic nature is regarded as
the root of the universe.

IT is everlasting and cannot be consumed.

## 無私章　第七

天長地久。
天地所以能長且久者，
以其不自生，故能長生。
是以聖人後其身而身先，
外其身而身存。
非以其無私邪？
故能成其私。

# CHAPTER SEVEN

Heaven is everlasting and earth is enduring.
    The reason that they are everlasting is because
    they do not exist for themselves.
    Hence, they are long lived.

Thus, although the saint puts himself last, finds himself in the lead.
Although he is not self-concerned, finds himself accomplished.
It is because he is not focused on self-interests and hence can
    fulfill his true nature.

道德經
TAO TE CHING

## 若水章 第八

上善若水。水善利萬物而不爭，處眾人之所惡，故幾於道。
居善地，心善淵，與善仁，言善信，正善治，事善能，動善時。
夫唯不爭，故無尤。

## CHAPTER EIGHT

A person of great virtue is like the flowing water.
Water benefits all things and contends not with them. It puts
    itself in a place that no one wishes to be and thus is

closest to TAO.

A virtuous person is like water which adapts
    itself to the perfect place.

His mind is like the deep water that is calm and peaceful.

His heart is kind like water that benefits all.

His words are sincere like the constant flow of water.

His governing is natural without desire which is like the softness of
    water that penetrates through hard rocks.

His work is of talent like the free flow of water.

His movement is of right timing like water that flows smoothly.

A virtuous person never forces his way and hence will not
    make faults.

道德經
TAO TE CHING

## 持盈章　第九

持而盈之，不如其已。
揣而銳之，不可長保。
金玉滿堂，莫之能守。
富貴而驕，自遺其咎。
功遂，身退，天之道。

## CHAPTER NINE

Those who overly pride wealth is like the overflowing water
   which shall cause damages. It is better to restrain early.

Those who are not content with fame is like polishing the edge of
   a knife. The sharper it gets, the easier it is to break.

Wealth and treasures are but illusions that one cannot possess.
Those who are arrogant of their wealth and fame shall invite blame
   upon oneself.

The nature TAO teaches one to retreat after one's success and
   not to hold on to the credit.

# 玄德章 第十

載營魄抱一，能無離乎？專氣致柔，能嬰兒乎？
滌除玄覽，能無疵乎？愛民治國，能無知乎？
天門開闔，能無雌乎？明白四達，能無爲乎？
生之，畜之。
生而不有，爲而不恃，長而不宰，是謂玄德。

# CHAPTER TEN

Can one unite the body and the spirit as one and embrace the
    "Oneness" without departing from the great TAO?
Can one achieve harmony with such gentleness by holding on
    to the true spirit within as if the innocence of an infant?
Can one free oneself from worldly knowledge and cleanse one's
    mind, so that no faults shall be made?
Can a ruler love his people by governing with the natural WAY
    without personal intention?
Can the mystic gate to all life essence be opened or closed
    without the virtue of the mysterious nature?
Can one gain the insight of nature and become a wise person
    without the effort of action?

The mysterious nature creates and nurtures all things
    without the desire to possess them.
IT performs with all efforts without claiming for credit.
IT flourishes all beings without the intention to take control of.
Such is the " Mystic TE " or " Mystic Virtue ".

# 虛中章 第十一

三十輻共一轂，當其無，有車之用。
埏埴以爲器，當其無，有器之用。
鑿戶牖以爲室，當其無，有室之用。
故有之以爲利，無之以爲用。

## CHAPTER ELEVEN

Thirty spokes unite around one hub to make a wheel.
It is the presence of the empty space that gives the function
    of a vehicle.
Clay is molded into a vessel. It is the empty space that gives the
    function of a vessel.
Doors and windows are chisel out to make a room.
    It is the empty space in the room that gives its function.

Therefore, something substantial can be beneficial.
While the emptiness of void is what can be utilized.

# 爲腹章 第十二

五色令人目盲；五音令人耳聾；五味令人口爽；
馳騁畋獵，令人心發狂；難得之貨，令人行妨。
是以聖人爲腹不爲目，故去彼取此。

## CHAPTER TWELVE

The five colors can blind one's eyes.

The five tones can deafen one's ears.

The five flavors can dull one's taste buds.

The pursuit of pleasures can derange one's mind.

The hard-to-get valuables can distort one's behavior.

Therefore, a saint cultivates himself with virtues and
    does not indulge himself in sensory pleasures.

He rejects those outer temptations and chooses this True Nature.

The greatest wisdom of Lao-Tze

道德經

TAO TE CHING

# 寵辱章 第十三

寵辱若驚，貴大患若身。何謂寵辱若驚？寵為下。得之若
驚，失之若驚，是謂寵辱若驚。何謂貴大患若身？吾所以
有大患者，為吾有身，及吾無身，吾有何患？故貴以身為
天下，若可寄天下；愛以身為天下，若可託天下。

## CHAPTER THIRTEEN

Honor and disgrace can surprise a person.
The greatest distress lies in one's physical body.

What does it mean by " Honor and disgrace can surprise someone? "
    Honor is inferior, because one who wins the favor is afraid of
    losing it. And one who loses the favor is frightened with distress.
This is the significance of " Honor and disgrace can surprise someone."

What does it mean by " The greatest distress lies in one's body? "
We have fear because we worry about our physical self. If one's body
    does not exist, how can one has fear?

Therefore, he who values the world as much as he values himself,
    can be entrusted with the ruling of the world.
He who loves the world as much as he loves himself,
    can be entrusted with the guidance of the world.

TAO TE CHING

# 道紀章 第十四

視之不見，名曰夷，聽之不聞，名曰希，搏之不得，名曰微。
此三者，不可致詰，故混而為一。
其上不皦，其下不昧，繩繩不可名，復歸於無物，
是謂無狀之狀，無物之象，是謂惚恍。
迎之不見其首，隨之不見其後。
執古之道，以御今之有。能知古始，是謂道紀。

# CHAPTER FOURTEEN

What cannot be seen is called the invisible.

What cannot be heard is called the inaudible.

What cannot be touched is called the intangible.

These three cannot be examined and comprehended.

And hence are mixed together as one.

This " Oneness " is not much brighter in the sky,
    as IT is not much dimmer on earth.

IT is not more glorious in a saint as IT is not more
    fainter in an ordinary person.

IT is everlasting and cannot be named.

IT is the original void of " non-being ".

This " Oneness " is the TAO which is invisible, and formless.
    IT may be regarded as vague and intangible.

When the Oneness TAO comes forward, ITs front cannot be seen.

When one tries to follow IT, one cannot see ITs rear.

By abiding with the original TAO, one can master the presence.

He who knows this " Origin ", shall know the teaching and
    principle of the Great TAO.

## 不盈章 第十五

古之善爲士者，微妙玄通，深不可識。夫唯不可識，故強爲之容：
豫焉，若冬涉川，猶兮，若畏四鄰。儼兮，其若客，渙兮，若冰之
將釋。敦兮，其若樸，曠兮，其若谷。混兮，其若濁。孰能濁以
止，靜之徐清，孰能安以久，動之徐生。保此道者，不欲盈。夫唯
不盈，故能蔽不新成。

# CHAPTER FIFTEEN

The ancient TAO cultivators were subtle and mysterious.
They were of immeasurable profundity.
Because they were too subtle to be known, so reluctantly
they were being described as follow :

Cautious, as if crossing an icy river.
Hesitant, as if fearful of the surroundings.
Reverent, like an honorable guest.
Dispersed, like winter ice began to melt in spring.
Simple and sincere, like a genuine virgin.
Open-minded, like an empty valley.
Harmonized, like the turbid water.

How can one turn the turbid water into clarity?
A person of TAO would maintain peace in order to achieve
pureness of the mind. And therefore shall not be disturbed
by the worldly desires.

After achieving pureness of the mind, how can one let it be
everlasting?
A person of TAO would unify and harmonize himself with
all beings which shall lead to eternity.

Those who abide by this TAO will not indulge themselves in the
desire of greed.
It is because of this humbleness that enables one to embrace the
original "ONENESS ", the Great TAO.

# 復命章 第十六

致虛極，守靜篤。萬物並作，吾以觀復。夫物芸芸，各復歸其根。歸根曰靜，是謂復命。復命曰常。知常曰明，不知常，妄作凶。知常容，容乃公，公乃王，王乃天。天乃道，道乃久，沒身不殆。

# CHAPTER SIXTEEN

Human must achieve the ultimate void and maintain calmness
    with sincerity in order to observe the growth and flourish
    of all beings.
It is in this way that one can understand the law of nature.

All things and beings will eventually return to the original source.
    This is called " peace ".
" Peace " means returning to one's original nature.
This original nature is the eternal law. To know the nature's law is to
    be enlightened.

He who is ignorant of the nature's law shall act recklessly, and thus
    will invite misfortune.

To know the constant law of nature is to be generous.
Being generous, one is impartial.
Being impartial, one is the sovereign.
Sovereign is the nature itself.
Nature is TAO.  TAO is everlasting.
When one's physical body dies away, TAO still long endures.

# 知有章　第十七

太上，下知有之；其次，親而譽之；其次，畏之；其次，侮之。
信不足焉，有不信焉。悠兮其貴言。
功成，事遂，百姓皆謂：我自然。

## CHAPTER SEVENTEEN

In early ancient mankind, TAO has been in existence in one's true
 nature. Men possess IT without knowing.

One then acts with virtue and honor which is inferior to TAO.
 The less superior is to act with fear.
 And the least superior is to act with disgrace .
This occurs because one does not have enough faith,
 and hence has no confidence.

The nature of TAO is distinguished by wordless teaching with the
 natural act of virtue without action.
As such, people would act effortlessly and harmonize with the
 Nature TAO.

## 四有章 第十八

大道廢，有仁義。
慧智出，有大偽。
六親不和，有孝慈。
國家昏亂，有忠臣。

道德經
TAO TE CHING

## CHAPTER  EIGHTEEN

When Great TAO declines, virtue of humanity and
    righteousness shall arise.

When knowledge and intelligence appear,
    great hypocrisy shall arise.

When the six various family relationships are not in harmony,
    filial piety and compassion shall arise.

When a country is in chaos, the loyal officials shall appear.

## 樸素章 第十九

絕聖棄智，民利百倍；絕仁棄義，民復孝慈；
絕巧棄利，盜賊無有。
此三者，以爲文，不足，故令有所屬：見素抱樸，少私寡欲。

## CHAPTER NINETEEN

Transcend the saint's teaching and conceal one's wisdom for
　　potential use, shall benefit the people a hundred fold.
Extend kindness to its ultimate and then polish to refine one's
　　righteousness shall help the people to regain filial piety
　　and compassion.

Employ one's subtle true nature with exquisiteness and extend one's
personal benefit to share with others, shall eliminate
robbers and thieves.

These three statements are apparent superficial and not sufficient
to express the natural " WAY " of the great TAO.

Hence, this is what people should do :
Return to their original true self and embrace the pure
" Oneness ".
Refrain selfishness and diminish worldly desires.

## 食母章 第二十

絕學無憂。唯之與阿，相去幾何？善之與惡，相去何若？

人之所畏，不可不畏，荒兮其未央哉！

眾人熙熙，如享太牢，如春登臺。

我獨泊兮其未兆，如嬰兒之未孩。

儽儽兮，若無所歸。眾人皆有餘，而我獨若遺。我愚人之心也哉！

沌沌兮，俗人昭昭，我獨昏昏。俗人察察，我獨悶悶。

澹兮其若海。飂兮若無止。眾人皆有以，而我獨頑且鄙。

我獨異於人，而貴食母。


## CHAPTER TWENTY

Enlightenment of the absolute TAO
> can free a person from worries and sorrow.

How much is the difference between a respectful response and
> an angry response?

How great is the difference between good and evil?

What people naturally fear, one should also fear.

One's endless desire can result in neglegence of the true nature of life.

People like to pursue after excitement as if they were ascending
the terrace in spring and celebrate a sacrificial feast.

But I alone remain quiet and calm like an infant who is pure and
innocent.

And I alone appeared to be lost like one who has nowhere to go.

All people have a surplus, but I alone was simple and
left out like a fool.

People seemed bright and shrewd, while I seemed dull.

People like to dispute, while I alone remain quiet.

I am calm and peaceful like the boundless ocean.

I am open-hearted and free like the wind blowing high above
the sky without hindrance.

Everyone thinks of themselves as capable and outstanding while
I appeared unlearned.

I am the only one to be different from others for I value highly
the Great TAO and joyfully act accordingly.

# 從道章　第二十一

孔德之容，惟道是從。
道之爲物，惟恍惟惚。
惚兮恍兮，其中有象。
恍兮惚兮，其中有物。
窈兮冥兮，其中有精。
其精甚眞，其中有信。
自古及今，其名不去，以閱衆甫。
吾何以知衆甫之狀哉！以此。

# CHAPTER TWENTY-ONE

A man of great virtue is one who follows the nature way of TAO.
This " TAO " is vague and intangible. Yet, in the vague and void,
    there is image, there is substance.
Within the profound intangible, there is essence;
    This essence is genuine.
    In IT lies the great faith.

Since the beginning of the world, TAO has been in existence.
Only through IT that one can understand the origin of all beings.
How do I know that this is the true essence?
It is through this natural WAY.

# 抱一章 第二十二

曲則全，枉則直，窪則盈，敝則新，少則得，多則惑。是以聖人抱一爲天下式。不自見，故明；不自是，故彰；不自伐，故有功；不自矜，故長。夫唯不爭，故天下莫能與之爭。古之所謂曲則全者，豈虛言哉！誠全而歸之。

# CHAPTER TWENTY-TWO

To yield is to preserve the whole.

To be misjudged is to be straightened.

To be hollow is to be filled.

To be battered is to be renewed.

To be in need is to possess.

To be abundant is to be confused.


Therefore, the saint embraces the "Oneness " as a standard for the world.

The wise one is not prejudiced, hence he is enlightened.

The wise one is not self-opinioned, hence he is outstanding.

The wise one does not boast of himself, hence he shall
receive the credit.

The wise one does not praise his own deeds, hence can
long endure.


Because the wise one does not conflict with others and therefore
the world cannot contend against him.

Is it not true as the ancients say, " To yield is to preserve the whole? "

Thus the " Oneness " will be honored to him.

## 同道章 第二十三

希言自然。故飄風不終朝，驟雨不終日。孰爲此者？天地。
天地尚不能久，而況於人乎？故從事於道者，道者同於道；
德者同於德；失者同於失。
同於道者，道亦樂得之；同於德者，德亦樂得之；
同於失者，失亦樂得之。信不足焉，有不信焉。

# CHAPTER TWENTY-THREE

Words that cannot be heard of are natural.

A gale can not blow for the whole morning.

A rainstorm cannot last for the whole day.

What caused these effects?

Heaven and earth.


Even the actions of nature do not last long.

How much more can human's behavior last when digressed from
    the natural TAO?

Thus, one who follows the Great TAO,

    when TAO is present, he will benefit the world with TAO.

    When TE is present, he will benefit the world with TE.

    When TAO and TE are both lost, he identifies himself with the
    people and benefits them with the enlightenment of teaching.


One who identifies with TAO is glad to be with TAO.

One who identifies with TE is glad to be with TE.

One who identifies with the loss of TAO and TE is
    glad to be with the lost.


If one does not have enough faith in " TAO ", how can
    he assist others to practice with faith?

# 不處章　第二十四

企者不立，跨者不行。自見者不明，自是者不彰，自伐
者無功，自矜者不長。其於道也，曰：餘食贅行，物或
惡之，故有道者不處。

## CHAPTER TWENTY-FOUR

He who raises himself on tiptoe cannot stand firm.
He who walks with strides cannot travel far.
He who is self-opinioned shall not be enlightened.
He who is prejudiced shall not be recognized.
He who brags about himself shall not receive credit.
He who is arrogant shall not make improvements.

In view of TAO, people who are self-centered are like
　　the surplus food and redundant actions in everyday life.
All things disgust them. Therefore a person of TAO
　　will not conduct himself in such manner.

# 混成章 第二十五

有物混成，先天地生。
寂兮寥兮，獨立不改，周行而不殆。可以爲天下母。
吾不知其名，字之曰道，強爲之名曰大。
大曰逝，逝而遠，遠曰反。
故道大，天大，地大，王亦大。
域中有四大，而王居其一焉。
人法地，地法天，天法道，道法自然。

# CHAPTER   TWENTY-FIVE

Something is formed in the chaos, which existed before
    heaven and earth.
IT is quiet and profound.
IT stands alone and alters not.
IT revolves eternally without exhaustion.
IT is regarded as the Mother of all beings.

I do not know ITs name, except to call IT " TAO ".
When forced to give IT a name, I would call IT " THE  GREAT ".
THE GREAT is far-reaching. Far-reaching is infinite.
Infinite is to return to the self-sufficient origin.

Therefore, " TAO " is great, heaven is great, earth is great,
    and so is the true-self.
There are four greatness in the universe, and true-self is one of them.

Man models the WAY of earth;
Earth models the WAY of heaven;
Heaven models the WAY of TAO;
TAO models the WAY of nature.

# 輜重章 第二十六

重爲輕根，靜爲躁君。
是以聖人終日行不離輜重。雖有榮觀，燕處超然。
奈何萬乘之主而以身輕天下？輕則失本，躁則失君。

## CHAPTER TWENTY-SIX

The heavy is the fundamental of the light.
Tranquility is the master of agitation.

Therefore, the saint always conducts himself with the essence
    of TAO and never departs from IT.
Although he is surrounded by the splendor of wealth,
    he remains to live a simple and ordinary life.

How can a ruler govern a nation without recklessness
    if he indulges in power and desire?
He who acts recklessly shall lose the essence of TAO.
He who is agitated with lust and desires shall lose his true nature.

寒山拾得為普賢
文殊菩薩之化身
今稱和聖合聖為
寒山拾得～來相也
乙丑年仲夏歲月間人
一師王樂寬書

# 襲明章 第二十七

善行無轍迹，善言無瑕讁，善數不用籌策，
善閉無關楗而不可開，善結無繩約而不可解。
是以聖人常善救人，故無棄人；常善救物，故無棄物。是謂
襲明。故善人者，不善人之師，不善人者，善人之資，
不貴其師，不愛其資，雖智大迷，是謂要妙。

## CHAPTER TWENTY-SEVEN

Good deeds leave no signs.

Good words leave no flaws.

Good scheme needs no deliberate plans.

A good lock uses no bolts, yet it cannot be opened.

A good knot uses no rope, yet it cannot be untied.

Hence, a saint is always kind by saving other people and rejects no one.

He is always kind by saving all things and therefore nothing is being
    rejected.

This is the true enlightenment.

Thus, a kind person is the teacher of the unkind.

An unkind person is a lesson for the kind to learn.

He who does not value his teacher and dislikes the valuable lesson,
    although knowledgeable, is in fact greatly confused.

This is the fundamental essence.

## 常德章　第二十八

知其雄，守其雌，為天下谿。為天下谿，常德不離，復歸於嬰兒。
知其白，守其黑，為天下式。為天下式，常德不忒，復歸於無極。
知其榮，守其辱，為天下谷。為天下谷，常德乃足，復歸於樸。
樸散則為器。聖人用之，則為官長。故大制不割。

# CHAPTER TWENTY-EIGHT

To know the strong masculine principle, yet abide by the gentle
    female principle is like being the valley of the world where
    all rivers will flow into.
This is alike all virtue which will merge into the subtle TAO.
Being a valley of the world and not depart from the true nature,
    one can return to original pureness like an infant.

When one knows the white that is splendor, yet holds on to the black
    that is humble and lowly. He can be a standard of the world.
Being a standard of the world and not deviate from true nature,
    one is able to return to the void of TAO.

To know what is honor, yet abide by the dishonored,
    is like a valley of the world which is modest and humble.
Being the valley of the world makes possible the true virtue to be
    complete and sufficient. And hence can return to simplicity.
When the nature of simplicity is being manifested, it results into
    various vessels.
And by applying the pure simplicity, a saint can master all things.
Hence, the Great TAO is a unified ONENESS which cannot be
    separated apart.

# 自然章 第二十九

將欲取天下而爲之，吾見其不得已。
天下神器，不可爲也。爲者敗之，執者失之。
故物或行或隨，或歔或吹，或強或羸，或載或隳。
是以聖人去甚，去奢，去泰。

## CHAPTER TWENTY-NINE

He who wishes to take control of the world and acts upon it,
  I can see that he will not succeed.

For the world is a divine vessel, it cannot be acted upon as one wish.

He who acts on it fails.

He who holds on to it loses.

Therefore some things move forward while some follow behind.

Some try to warm with exhaled air while some try to blow it cold.

Some are strong while some are weak.

Some are successfully accomplished while some are declined
        and failed.

Thus, the saint avoids all extremes, extravagance, and pride.

## 不道章　第三十

以道佐人主者，
不以兵強天下，
其事好還。
師之所處，
荊棘生焉，
大軍之後，
必有凶年。
善有果而已，
不敢以取強。
果而勿矜，
果而勿伐，
果而勿驕。
果而不得已，
果而勿強。
物壯則老，
是謂不道，
不道早已。

道德經　TAO TE CHING

# CHAPTER THIRTY

One who assists the ruler with the principle of TAO,
      will not use the force of arms to conquer the world.
For such affairs will result in cause and effect.
Wherever the armies touch the land, it is turned into
      a wasteland of thorns and brambles.
After a war is fought, bad years are sure to follow.

Therefore, one who follows the true nature will understand the
      principle of cause and effect and shall not rely upon the
      strength of force.

By knowing the effect, thus one will not brag.
By knowing the effect, thus one will not boast.
By knowing the effect, thus one will not become arrogant.
By knowing the effect, although one has no choice, one still
      abides with the principle of cause and effect and does not
      resolve into force.

When things reach their prime, they start to age and decline.
This is the life that is diminishing and shall not reach the
      ultimate essence.

# 貴左章　第三十一

夫佳兵者不祥之器，物或惡之，故有道者不處。

君子居則貴左，用兵則貴右，

兵者不祥之器，非君子之器，不得已而用之，恬淡爲上。

勝而不美，而美之者，是樂殺人。

夫樂殺人者，則不可以得志於天下矣。

吉事尙左，凶事尙右。偏將軍居左，上將軍居右。言以喪禮處之。

殺人之衆，以悲哀泣之，戰勝則以喪禮處之。


## CHAPTER THIRTY-ONE

Weapons of war are instruments of disaster.

    They are rejected by all beings.

    Thus a person of TAO will not dwell upon them.

According to the ancient custom of Ying and Yang,

    a man of virtue values the left which is represented by Yang.

    And a man of war values the right which is represented

    by Ying.

Weapons are instruments of evil, and are not valued by a man
of virtue.
They are only used as the last resort to attain peace when all
else have failed.
If their use is necessary, it is best to employ with calmness and
tranquility.
Even if it means victory, it is not something pleasant.
Those who rejoice over the victory, enjoy killing.
He who delights in killing will not be favored by the
people and  shall not bring harmony to the world.

It is the ancient custom to favor happy events to the left as
represented by Yang. While on sad occasions, it is favored to
the right as represented by Ying.
When this rite is applied in the army, the lieutenant general takes
the place of the left, and the commander-in-chief takes the
place of the right.
This indicates that war is treated as if it's a funeral service;
for many lives had been killed and hence should be mourned
with sorrow.

Therefore, although a victory was won, it is treated like a funeral rite.

TAO TE CHING

## 知止章　第三十二

道常無名樸，雖小，天下莫能臣也。侯王若能守之，萬物將自賓。天地相合，以降甘露，民莫之令而自均。始制有名，名亦旣有，夫亦將知止，知止可以不殆。譬道之在天下，猶川谷之與江海。

# CHAPTER THIRTY-TWO

The universal TAO has no name.
Although IT appears in the plainest and may seem small, IT
    is inferior to nothing.

If the kings and marquises can abide by the Great TAO,
    all beings shall act as guests and submit to them.
Heaven and earth will then be in harmony and shall descend
    sweet dew.
People will not require command and orders,
    yet can treat each other equally with peace.

When " TAO " is manifested, names were given for the purpose
    of distinction.
But one must know how to attain the original pureness in order to
    avoid danger and disaster.

TAO exists in the universe like the rivers and streams that lead
    to the ocean.

道德經
TAO TE CHING

# 盡己章 第三十三

知人者智，自知者明。勝人者有力，自勝者強。
知足者富。強行者有志。不失其所者久。死而不亡者壽。

## CHAPTER THIRTY-THREE

One who knows other people is wise.

One who knows himself is enlightened.

To overcome others is strong.

To overcome oneself is the will of power.

One who is contented is rich.

One who is determined has the strength of will.

Those who embrace their true nature shall long live.

He who is enlightened with the original nature, although dies
  physically, is eternally united with the everlasting TAO.

# 成大章　第三十四

大道氾兮，其可左右。
萬物恃之而生而不辭。
功成不名有，衣養萬物而不爲主。
常無欲，可名於小；
萬物歸焉而不爲主，可名爲大。
以其終不自爲大，故能成其大。

## CHAPTER THIRTY-FOUR

The great TAO is ever present.
IT can adjust ITSELF to everything.

All things live by IT, and IT does not deny them.

When ITs work is accomplished, IT does not claim possession.

IT gives great love to nurture all things and all lives, but
     dominates  not.

The true void of TAO has no desires and may seem small.

Yet all things entrust their lives to IT and IT does not act as
     their master.

This may be recognized as " The Great ".

Because a saint does not restrict himself with the greatness,
     hence his greatness is accomplished.

## 大象章 第三十五

執大象，天下往。
往而不害，安平太。
樂與餌，過客止。
道之出口，
淡乎其無味，
視之不足見，
聽之不足聞，
用之不足既。

# CHAPTER THIRTY-FIVE

He who embraces the Great TAO shall be the guidance of the world.

By following him, the world will not be harmed and will be rendered
with peace and harmony.

Pleasures and delicacy can only attract passers-by to stay temporarily.

The teaching of TAO is plain without extraordinary appearances.

IT can not be seen,

IT can not be heard,

IT can not be depleted or exhausted.

# 微明章　第三十六

將欲歙之，必固張之。將欲弱之，必固強之。
將欲廢之，必固興之。將欲奪之，必固與之。是謂微明。
柔弱勝剛強。魚不可脫於淵。國之利器不可以示人。

## CHAPTER　THIRTY-SIX

If desire shall conceal true self,

　　true self will manifest itself even more.

If desire shall weaken true self,

　　true self will strengthen itself even more.

If desire shall abandon true self,

　　true self will prosperous even more.

If desire shall deprive true self,

　　true self will give even more.


This is known as the enlightened nature that is subtle yet profound.

Gentleness overcomes strength, and the meek overcomes the strong.

Just as fish live in deep water and cannot survive after being

　　taken out of the depths.

And the powerful weapons of a country should not be displayed,

　　just like one's true nature cannot be revealed to be seen.

# 無爲章 第三十七

道常無爲，而無不爲。侯王若能守之，萬物將自化。
化而欲作，吾將鎮之以無名之樸。
無名之樸，夫亦將無欲。不欲以靜，天下將自定。

## CHAPTER THIRTY-SEVEN

The everlasting TAO acts according to the natural WAY.

Therefore there is nothing that IT will not accomplish.

If kings and the nobilities can abide by their true nature and follow
     the great TAO, all things shall be reformed naturally.

If during the process of reform, desires arouse,

I shall overcome with the simplicity of original nature.

With the simplicity of true nature, there shall be no desire.

Without desire, one's original nature will be at peace.

And the world will naturally be in accord with the right " WAY ".

# 處厚章　第三十八

上德不德，是以有德。下德不失德，是以無德。
上德無爲而無以爲。下德爲之而有以爲。
上仁爲之而無以爲。上義爲之而有以爲。
上禮爲之而莫之應，則攘臂而扔之。
故失道而後德，失德而後仁，失仁而後義，失義而後禮。
夫禮者，忠信之薄，而亂之首。前識者，道之華，而愚之始。
是以大丈夫處其厚，不居其薄，處其實，不居其華。故去彼取此。

## CHAPTER  THIRTY-EIGHT

A man of superior virtue is not conscious of being virtuous,
　　hence is truly virtuous.
A man of inferior virtue performs for the purpose of virtue,
　　hence he is not virtuous.
A man of superior virtue acts without action,
　　and performs with his true nature.
A man of inferior virtue acts with intentional effort.

A man of superior kindness acts a natural act.

A man of superior justice acts with righteousness and feelings
for others.

A man of superior etiquette acts according to his true self,
hence no one responds to him by moving away.


Therefore, when " TAO " is lost, there is TE ( virtue ).

When TE is lost, there is humanity.

When humanity is lost, there is justice.

When justice is lost, there is etiquette.

Etiquette becomes prevalent when people fail to be sincere and honest.

Hence, chaos begins.


A person of knowledge and self-opinion will be hindered from the
enlightenment of TAO.
Thus, this is the beginning of ignorance!

Therefore, one who cultivates himself with TAO, embraces the
original nature and indulges not in sensual nature.
He abides by the fundamental Oneness and indulges not
in sensory pleasures.

Thus, abandon those desires and abide by this true essence of TAO.

# 得一章 第三十九

昔之得一者，天得一以清，地得一以寧，神得一以靈，
谷得一以盈，萬物得一以生，侯王得一以爲天下貞。
其致之，天無以清將恐裂，地無以寧將恐發，神無以靈將恐歇，
谷無以盈將恐竭，萬物無以生將恐滅，侯王無以貴高將恐蹶。
故貴以賤爲本，高以下爲基。
是以侯王自謂孤寡不穀，此非以賤爲本邪？非乎？
故致數輿無輿，不欲琭琭如玉，珞珞如石。

## CHAPTER THIRTY-NINE

In the beginning, there were those who attained the " ONENESS ";

Heaven, by attaining the Oneness became clear;

Earth, by attaining the Oneness became peaceful;

Spirit, by attaining the Oneness became divine;

True nature is like an empty valley, and by attaining the Oneness,

　　IT became fully productive.

All things, by attaining the Oneness became alive.

Emperors and nobilities, by attaining " Oneness"  can bring
    peace and prosperity to the world.
All these are the results of achieving " ONENESS ".

Heaven, without clarity would crack.
Earth, without peace would quake.
Spirit, without divinity would be powerless.
True nature, without productivity would result in exhaustion of life.
All things, without life essence would perish.
Emperors, without "Oneness"  to exalt them to nobility, would
    stumble and fall.
Thus, honor is based on humbleness.

The high builds its foundation upon the low.
Therefore, the kings and nobles call themselves " The solitude ",
    " The unworthy ", " The virtueless ".
Is this not the reason why they base their honor upon humbleness?
Hence, the highly honored do not regard themselves as nobles and
    have no wish to be self-centered to think nobly of themselves
    as a piece of jade nor to think lowly of others as a lump
    of stone.

道德經 TAO TE CHING

## 反覆章 第四十

反者，道之動。
弱者，道之用。
天下萬物生於有，
有生於無。

# CHAPTER FORTY

When TAO is in action, one's worldly nature can be reversed to
the true nature.

Gentleness is the way of application of TAO.

All things in the world originate from the manifestation of TAO,

The manifestation of TAO is the form of being, which originates
from the non-being of the void, the Great TAO.

# 聞道章 第四十一

上士聞道，勤而行之；中士聞道，若存若亡；下士聞道，大笑之。不笑，不足以爲道。故建言有之：明道若昧，進道若退，夷道若類，上德若谷，大白若辱，廣德若不足，建德若偸，質眞若渝，大方無隅，大器晚成，大音希聲，大象無形，道隱無名。夫唯道善貸且成。

# CHAPTER FORTY-ONE

When a superior man heard of TAO,
    he cultivates himself diligently.
When an average man heard of TAO,
    he is doubtful, vague and would give up halfway.
When an inferior man heard of TAO,
    he laughs and thinks of IT as foolish.

If TAO is not being laughed at, IT is not the "GREAT TAO".
Thus, there is a traditional saying of,
    one who is enlightened with TAO may appear foolish.
    He who is advancing in TAO may appear to withdraw.
Great TAO is plain and simple which can adapt to all
    circumstances, although IT may seem uneven and rough.

A man of superior virtue is like an empty, receptive valley.
A man of innocence may appear to be disgraced.
A man of great virtue appears to be deficient.
A man who practices TAO and actively achieves great merits
    may appear gentle and meek.
A man who follows his true self may appear to be changeable.

Generosity has no rough angles.
Great achievement is time consuming, and is slow to complete.
Great tone has no sound.
Great TAO is formless,
    IT is invisible and has no name.
    IT benefits all and fulfills all.

# 沖和章　第四十二

道生一，一生二，二生三，三生萬物。萬物負陰而抱陽，沖氣以為和。人之所惡，唯孤寡不穀，而王公以為稱。故物或損之而益，或益之而損。人之所教，我亦教之，強梁者不得其死，吾將以為教父。

## CHAPTER FORTY-TWO

TAO gives birth to one.

One gives birth to two.

Two gives birth to three.

Three gives birth to all things and all beings.

All beings bear the negative physical form which is
    represented by Ying, and embrace the positive true nature
    which is represented by Yang.

With the union of these two, they arrive at a state of harmony.


Men dislike to be " the solitude ", " the unworthy ", and
    "the virtueless ",
    yet the Lords and nobles call themselves these names.

Hence, things are benefitted by being humble,
    and damaged by profitting.


What the ancients had taught, I shall also teach as such:

A man of violence who is in disharmony between Ying and Yang
    that is the physical body and true self, shall die of an
    unnatural death.

This is the essential of my teaching.

# 至柔章 第四十三

天下之至柔，馳騁天下之至堅。無有入無間。吾是以知無爲之有
益。不言之敎，無爲之益，天下希及之。

## CHAPTER FORTY-THREE

The softest of all things can overcome the hardest of all things.

Regardless of being or the non-being, they all have to return to the
　　empty void to express their gentleness.

Thus, I have learned the benefits of natural actions without
　　personal desires.

Very few can understand the value of wordless teaching and the
　　act of natural " WAY ".

## 知止章　第四十四

名與身孰親？身與貨孰多？得與亡孰病？
是故甚愛必大費，多藏必厚亡。
知足不辱　，知止不殆，可以長久。

# CHAPTER  FORTY-FOUR

Fame and life, which one is of intimacy?
Life and wealth, which one is of importance?
To gain one but to lose the other, which is of harm?

Therefore, if one's desires are great, one would result in exhaustion.
Overstock shall result in heavy loss.
He who is contented will not suffer disgrace.
He who knows his true nature will not incur danger.

It is in this " WAY " that one can long endure.

# 清靜章　第四十五

大成若缺，其用不弊；大盈若沖，其用不窮。
大直若屈，大巧若拙，大辯若訥。
躁勝寒，靜勝熱，清靜爲天下正。

# CHAPTER  FORTY-FIVE

Great achievement appears to be inadequate, yet its use is never
    exhausted.

Great fullness appears to be void, yet its use is boundless.

Great honesty may seem to be accused of wrong doing.

Great mastery appears to be clumsy.

Great eloquence may seem to be inarticulate.

Movement can overcome chill.

Tranquility can overcome heat.

Peace and calmness is the " WAY " to guide the world.

孝女將軍花木蘭

# 知足章 第四十六

天下有道，卻走馬以糞；天下無道，戎馬生於郊，
罪莫大於可欲；禍莫大於不知足；咎莫大於欲得。
故知足之足，常足矣。

## CHAPTER FORTY-SIX

When the world lives in accord with TAO,
    fine walking horses can be retired from plowing the field.

When the world fails to live in accord with TAO,
    even pregnant mares are used as war horses,
    and were forced to breed in the battlefield.

The greatest crime is to have too much desire.
The greatest disaster is not to find contentment.
The greatest mistake is to desire for endless possession.

Hence, when one is gratified with self-contentment,
    true contentment can then long endure.

道德經

TAO TE CHING

# 天道章 第四十七

不出戶，知天下；不闚牖，見天道。其出彌遠，其知彌少。
是以，聖人不行而知，不見而名，不為而成。

## CHAPTER FORTY-SEVEN

TAO exists in one's own true self.

IT cannot be found outside of one's true nature.

Hence, there is no need to leave the house to take a journey
in order to know the world.

There is no need to look outside of the window to see the
nature of TAO.

The further one departs from TAO, the less one will be able
to know.

Therefore a saint is wise to know without seeking for IT.

He is wise to understand without seeing IT.

He is wise to accomplish according to the Natural " WAY ".

# 日損章 第四十八

爲學日益，爲道日損。損之又損，以至於無爲，無爲而無不爲。
取天下常以無事，及其有事，不足以取天下。

## CHAPTER FORTY-EIGHT

In pursuing knowledge,
    one learns with intellect and desires, therefore
    one's knowledge is accumulated day after day.

In pursuing TAO,
    one is enlightened with the true nature and thus
    diminishes daily one's worldly desires and knowledge.

The continuous depletion of one's desires persists
    until one acts accordingly to the natural " WAY ".
By acting without personal intention enables one to accomplish
    all things.

Therefore, to rule over the world,
    one must act naturally without personal desires.
If one pursues with extreme effort, one shall fail to rule the world.

# 道善章　第四十九

聖人無常心，以百姓心爲心。
善者，吾善之，不善者，吾亦善之，德善。
信者，吾信之，不信者，吾亦信之，德信。
聖人在天下，歙歙爲天下渾其心。百姓皆注其耳目，聖人皆孩之。

## CHAPTER　FORTY-NINE

The saint has no set mind,

 he regards the wish of the people as his own wish.

 He is kind to the kind, he is also kind to the unkind.

 This is the true virtue of kindness.

The saint trusts those who are trustworthy.

 He also trusts those who are not trustworthy.

 This is the true virtue of trust .

The saint conducts himself in the world by harmonizing with

 all beings to be at one.

The worldly people thus look up to him attentively with their

 eyes and ears.

And the saint treats the people like a loving mother who loves

 her children unconditionally.

## 生死章　第五十

出生入死。生之徒十有三，死之徒十有三，人之生，動之死地，亦
十有三。夫何以故？以其生生之厚。蓋聞善攝生者，陸行不遇兕
虎，入軍不被甲兵。兕無所投其角，虎無所措其爪，兵無所容其
刃，夫何故？以其無死地。

## CHAPTER　FIFTY

Men enter this world with life and leave this world with death.
Those who work hard for living and longevity are comprised of
   one-third of the people.

Those who are leading their life towards death are comprised of
another one-third.
Those who live with indulgence in passion and desires shall harm
their life and invite death. This is comprised of
the final one-third of the people.
Why is this so?
It's because men are over-concerned with pleasures of life and
hence exhaust themselves with hard work of desires of greed.

The wise one who knows how to nourish life with the Nature
TAO, when he travels, will not encounter fierce animals
such as wild buffalos and tigers.
When he is engaged in the battlefield, will not be harmed
by the weapons.
The horns of the wild buffalos are powerless against him.
The claws of the tigers are useless against him.
The weapons are of no avail towards him.

Why is this so?
It's because the wise one follows the great TAO and cultivates
himself accordingly.
Hence, a man of TAO will not perish.

126

# 尊貴章 第五十一

道生之，德畜之，物形之，勢成之。是以萬物莫不尊道而貴德。道之尊，德之貴，夫莫之命而常自然。故道生之，德畜之，長之、育之、亭之、毒之、養之、覆之。生而不有，爲而不恃，長而不宰，是謂玄德。

## CHAPTER FIFTY-ONE

TAO gives birth to all things.
And TE ( virtue ) nurtures them.
Matter shapes them.
The natural environment matures them.

Therefore, all things abide by TAO and honor TE.
Although TAO deserves reverence and TE deserves honor,
　　they are not demanded by decree,
　　　but is a result of the NATURE WAY.
Hence, TAO gives life to all beings and TE nurtures, grows,
　　fosters, develops, matures, supports and protects them.

TAO gives birth to life and yet claims no possession.
IT gives support without holding on to the merit.
IT matures them but does not take control of.
This is called the Mystic TE.

## 守母章 第五十二

天下有始，以爲天下母。

旣得其母，以知其子；旣知其子，復守其母，沒身不殆。

塞其兌，閉其門，終身不勤；

開其兌，濟其事，終身不救。

見小曰明，守柔曰強。用其光，復歸其明。

無遺身殃，是爲習常。

# CHAPTER FIFTY-TWO

The beginning of the universe is TAO,

IT is the mother of all.

By knowing the Mother, we will know her creations.

By knowing the creation of all lives, one can then return to the origin
and abide by the Mother.

It is in this way that although the body dies, the spiritual nature
will not perish.


To abide by the Mother of TAO is to keep guard on one's sensory
desire and shut the doors of temptation so as to prevent
one from pursuing outwards.

Thus, by doing so one's whole life may be preserved from exhaustion
and pains.

However, if on the contrary one indulges oneself in the pleasure of
desire and opens the door of temptation to pursue outwards,
then one's true nature will be lost and hence is beyond rescuing.


Those who are aware of the essence of the original nature are said
to be enlightened.

Those who abide by the gentleness of TAO are said to be strong.

Those who employ the glory of TAO,
and were able to return to the true nature, are ensured of no
distress and is said to embrace the Nature TAO.

The greatest wisdom of Lao-Tze

道德經

TAO-TE-CHING

# 大道章 第五十三

使我介然有知，行於大道，惟施是畏。
大道甚夷，而民好徑。朝甚除，田甚蕪，倉甚虛；
服文綵，帶利劍，厭飲食，財貨有餘，是謂盜夸，非道也哉！

## CHAPTER FIFTY-THREE

If I were to have the very slight insight,

I would live in accordance with the Great TAO.

My only fear is, to go astray from TAO while spreading IT.

Great TAO is smooth and plain, yet people prefer the devious
bypaths.

Hence, the government is corrupted with luxury and splendor.
The people were exhausted with labor and left the fields to be
wasted and the granaries depleted.

Under such practices, the officials would wear fine clothes, carry
sharp swords and indulge themselves in good food and drinks.
They crave with greed to possess great wealth.

Such is said to commit the crime of robbery and certainly is not
the WAY of TAO.

## 善建章 第五十四

善建者不拔，善抱者不脫，子孫以祭祀不輟。
修之於身，其德乃眞；修之於家，其德乃餘；
修之於鄉，其德乃長；修之於國，其德乃豐；
修之於天下，其德乃普。故以身觀身，
以家觀家，以鄉觀鄉，以國觀國，以天下觀天下。
吾何以知天下之然哉？以此。

# CHAPTER FIFTY-FOUR

One who cultivates himself with TAO, firmly establishes his virtue.
He holds on faithfully to the Great Oneness, and is honored for
generations ever after.

Cultivate oneself with the Oneness, TAO
and the virtue is genuine.
Cultivate a family with the Oneness, TAO
and the virtue is in surplus.
Cultivate an entire village with the Oneness, TAO
and the virtue is enduring.
Cultivate a whole nation with the Oneness, TAO
and the virtue is luxuriant.
Cultivate the whole world with the Oneness, TAO
and the virtue is universal.

Hence, by cultivating oneself, thus gains insight into one's true virtue.
By cultivating a family, thus gains insight into a loving family.
By cultivating a village, thus gains insight into a harmonious village.
By cultivating a nation, thus gains insight into the extensive benefits
for the people.
By cultivating the whole world, thus gains insight into the
universal peace that embrace all beings.

How do I know that the world is so?
It is through this WAY.

道德經 TAO TE CHING

## 含德章 第五十五

含德之厚，比於赤子。蜂蠆虺蛇不螫，猛獸不據，攫鳥不搏。骨弱筋柔而握固。未知牝牡之合而全作，精之至也。終日號而不嗄，和之至也。知和曰常。知常曰明。益生曰祥。心使氣曰強。物壯則老，謂之不道。不道早已。

# CHAPTER FIFTY--FIVE

One who preserves TE ( virtue ) in fullness,
    is to be compared to an innocent infant.
Hence, no poisonous insects will sting him.
    No wild beasts will attack him.
    No birds of prey will pounce upon him.

In governing one's life, learn from an infant as such:
    Its bones are soft, its tendons are tender, yet its grip is firm.
    Not knowing the unity of male and female,
    yet the infant's sexual organ is aroused.
This is because its life essence is pure and complete.
Crying all day, yet the infant's voice does not turn hoarse.
Such is the perfect harmony.

To know harmony is called " Everlasting ".
To know everlasting is called " Enlightenment ".
To overprotect one's life is called " Ill omen ".
To let one's mind follow the emotional impulse is called
    " Compulsion ".

When things reach their prime they start to age and decline.
This is the life that is diminishing, which shall not reach the
    ultimate essence.

# 道貴章 第五十六

知者不言，言者不知。塞其兌，閉其門，挫其銳，
解其紛，和其光，同其塵。是謂玄同。故不可得而親，不可得而疏；
不可得而利，不可得而害；不可得而貴，不可得而賤。故爲天下貴。

## CHAPTER  FIFTY-SIX

The wise does not speak.
He who speaks is not wise.

Keep silent and close one's mouth.
Keep guard on one's sensory organs.
Round off one's edges.
Untie the entangled.
Harmonize with the glory.
Mix with the lowliness.
This is called the Mystic Unity.

Because the wise is unified with all and has no distinction,
    thus, one cannot get close to him,
        nor can one keep far away from him,
        one cannot benefit him,
        nor can one harm him,
        one cannot honor him,
        nor can one disgrace him.
Therefore, he is honored by the whole world.

## 治國章 第五十七

以正治國，以奇用兵，以無事取天下。
吾何以知其然哉？以此。
天下多忌諱，而民彌貧；
民多利器，國家滋昏；
人多伎巧，奇物滋起；
法令滋彰，盜賊多有。
故聖人云：我無為而民自化；
我好靜而民自正；我無事而民自富；
我無欲而民自樸。

# CHAPTER FIFTY-SEVEN

Govern a nation with the right principle,
Fight a battle with the tactics of surprise,
Rule over the world with peace and natural effort.
How do I know that this is so? By the following:

The more prohibitions that are imposed on people,
    the poorer the people become.
The more sharp weapons the people possess,
    the greater is the chaos in the country.
The more clever and crafty the people become,
    the more unusual affairs occur.
The more laws and regulations that exist,
    the more thieves and brigands appear.

Hence, the saint declares:
    I act effortlessly with the WAY of TAO,
        thus, people transform themselves naturally.
    I love tranquility and peace,
        thus, people naturally follow the right WAY.
    I do not exhaust people with labor,
        thus, people naturally are wealthy.
    I have no personal desires,
        thus, people naturally are innocent and simple.

# 察政章 第五十八

其政悶悶，其民淳淳；其政察察，其民缺缺。
禍兮福之所倚，福兮禍之所伏。孰知其極？其無正。
正復爲奇，善復爲妖。人之迷，其日固久。
是以聖人方而不割，廉而不劌，直而不肆，光而不耀。

## CHAPTER FIFTY-EIGHT

When the government is dull, people are simple and sincere.
When the government is complex and stringent,
    people are cunning and shall cause trouble.

Calamity is what blessings depend upon.
In blessings there hides the calamity.
Who knows the ultimate end of the cycle of calamity and blessings?
Is there no true principle that exists?

The normal may revert and become unusual.
The good may revert and turn into evil.
Long indeed, man has been under such delusion.
Therefore, the saint abides by firm principle and does not depart
    from it.
He is honest and not mean.
He is upright and not rude.
He is honored and not eminent.

## 長生章 第五十九

治人事天莫若嗇。夫唯嗇，是謂早服；
早服謂之重積德；重積德則無不克；
無不克則莫知其極；莫知其極，可以有國；
有國之母，可以長久。
是謂深根固柢，長生久視之道。

## CHAPTER  FIFTY-NINE

In governing one's life and serving the nature,
there is nothing better than to follow the
WAY of simplicity.

Simplicity is to restrain one's desires.

To restrain one's desires is to practice the virtue of Nature WAY.

By practicing the virtue of Nature WAY,

   one is capable to accomplish anything.

With the ability to accomplish anything,

   one can achieve the infinite realm.

By achieving the infinite realm,

   one can then become a true leader of a nation.


To govern a nation with the Law of Nature is to be long enduring.

This is regarded as a profound and firm foundation of the

   everlasting TAO.

道德經
TAO-TE-CHING

# 治大國章　第六十

治大國若烹小鮮。以道蒞天下，其鬼不神；非其鬼不神，
其神不傷人；非其神不傷人，聖人亦不傷人。夫兩不相
傷，故德交歸焉。

## CHAPTER SIXTY

Ruling a great nation is like frying small fish.

    When they are over stirred, they will break into pieces.

Guide the world with TAO,

    then the spiritual beings would lose their power.

    It is in fact not that the spiritual beings had lost their power,

        but that their spiritual power will not harm people.

    It is in fact not that the spiritual power cannot harm people,

        but that the true nature of the saint has harmonized with

        the spiritual power and hence will cause no harm.

Since they both do not harm each other,

    therefore they will harmonize with the true virtue to embrace

    the ONENESS, TAO.

# 爲下章 第六十一

大國者下流，天下之交，天下之牝。
牝常以靜勝牡，以靜爲下。
故大國以下小國，則取小國；
小國以下大國，則取大國。
故或下以取，或下而取。
大國不過欲兼畜人，小國不過欲入事人。
夫兩者各得其所欲，大者宜爲下。

# CHAPTER SIXTY-ONE

A great nation rules by placing itself in a lowly position like the rivers
    that flow into the low regions of ocean.
Hence, people will naturally be faithful to their country.


Mother nature always stays calm and quiet to overcome
    the unrest.
IT takes the lowly position to be in peace.
Thus, if a great nation can lower itself to deal with a
        smaller nation, then it shall win the heart of the people. And
        the smaller nation will willingly merge with the great nation.
And if the smaller nation can lower itself to deal with the
        great nation, then it shall win the trust and be accommodated
        as a part of the great nation.


Therefore, be it to take a lowly position to win over or to take
        a lowly position to be accommodated;
        The great nation only wishes to unite and shelter all the
        people, while the small nation only wishes to be a part
        of the great nation to serve it.
Now that both are granted with what they wish for,
        it is only natural for the " Great " to put itself in a
        lowly position.

金鷄一鳴天下白
癸酉一九九三年仲春
陳慶如畫

# 道奧章　第六十二

道者，萬物之奧，善人之寶，不善人之所保。
美言可以市，尊行可以加人，人之不善，何棄之有？
故立天子，置三公，雖有拱璧以先駟馬，不如坐進此道。
古之所以貴此道者，何？不曰以求得，有罪以免邪？故為天下貴。

## CHAPTER SIXTY-TWO

TAO is the wonder of all creations.

IT is a treasure for those who are kind.

IT can also protect those who are not kind.


Words of TAO can benefit all people.

ITs action can guide people to follow the right WAY.

Those who have gone astray, the all-forgiving TAO will not
abandon them.

Therefore, it is better to embrace this precious TAO than to be
crowned as kings or appointed as ministers or to possess
wealth and fine horses.


So why did the ancients value and honor this TAO?

It is because " Those who seek will attain, those who
offended will be forgiven".

Thus, IT is the greatest honor in the world.

# 無難章 第六十三

爲無爲，事無事，味無味。
大小多少，報怨以德。
圖難於其易，爲大於其細。
天下難事必作於易，
天下大事必作於細。
是以聖人終不爲大，
故能成其大。
夫輕諾必寡信，
多易必多難。
是以聖人猶難之，
故終無難矣。

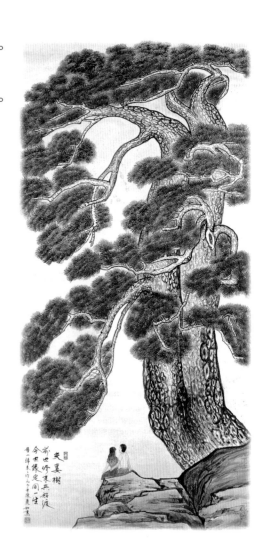

# CHAPTER SIXTY-THREE

Act without personal desire.

Manage without intentional concern.

Taste without desire of the flavor.

Hold the same regard for big or small, abundant or little and reward

     the unkind with kindness.


Plan for the difficult while it is easy.

Act upon the great from the beginning of the minute.

All difficult affairs must be taken care of when they are easy.

All great accomplishments must be performed from the small tasks.

Hence, a saint does not strive to do something great,

     and as a result he is able to accomplish the great.


He who makes promises easily seldom keeps his words.

He who constantly regards things as easy shall result in difficulty.

Therefore, the saint is aware of the difficulties ahead and hence

     is cautious in managing affairs while they are still easy and

     small to prevent resulting into problems.

## 輔物章 第六十四

其安易持，其未兆易謀，
其脆易泮，其微易散。
為之於未有，治之於未亂。
合抱之木生於毫末；
九層之臺起於累土；
千里之行始於足下。
為者敗之，執者失之。
是以聖人無為故無敗，
無執故無失。
民之從事常於幾成而敗之。
慎終如始，則無敗事。
是以聖人欲不欲，
不貴難得之貨；學不學，
復眾人之所過。
以輔萬物之自然，
而不敢為。

# CHAPTER SIXTY-FOUR

It is easy to preserve when things are stable.

It is easy to plan ahead when things have not yet occurred.

If one waits until the affair has begun,

    then the situation is as brittle as ice that easily cracks

    and is fragile that easily shatters.


Take actions before things occur.

Manage before things get out of order.

    A huge tree grows from a tiny sprout;

    A nine-story high terrace is built from heaps of earth.

    A journey of thousand miles begins from the first step.

He who acts with desire shall fail.

He who tries to possess shall lose.

Therefore, the saint acts without effort and so he does not fail.

    He is not eager to possess and so he does not lose.


Most people fail when they are near completion.

If one can be cautious from beginning to end, then he will not fail.

Thus a saint pursues what people do not pursue.

    He does not value the hard-to-get objects.

    He learns what people do not learn and avoids the

        faults in order to restore his true nature.

    He follows the course of nature to benefit all things

        and dares not go astray from the right WAY, TAO.

# 玄德章第六十五

古之善爲道者，非以明民，將以愚之。民之難治，以其智多。

故以智治國，國之賊；不以智治國，國之福。

知此兩者，亦稽式。常知稽式，是謂玄德。

玄德深矣，遠矣！與物反矣，然後乃至大順。

## CHAPTER SIXTY-FIVE

The ancient TAO cultivators,

> did not lead people to acquire knowledge to be tricky,
>
> but to guide them to restore their simplicity and innocence.

The reason people are difficult to be governed is because they are

> clever and witty.

Therefore, he who rules a nation with tactics and wits shall do harm

> to the country. He who does not rule with such is the nation's
>
> blessing.

To know these two principles is to know the rule of nature.

To know the rule of nature is called Mystic TE ( Mystic Virtue ).

Mystic TE is profound and far-reaching.

IT can guide all things to return to their original nature,

> and thus great harmony can be achieved.

## 江海章 第六十六

江海所以能爲百谷王者，
以其善下之，故能爲百谷王。
是以欲上民，必以言下之；
欲先民，必以身後之。
是以聖人處上，而民不重；
處前，而民不害。
是以天下樂推而不厭。
以其不爭，故天下莫能與之爭。

# CHAPTER SIXTY-SIX

The reason that river and ocean can be the Lords of all valley
    is because they are located in the lowly position.
Therefore, the saint humbles himself to serve all people.
    And he leads the people by putting himself last for the sake
    of the people's welfare.
Thus, although he rules above the people,
    the people do not feel him as a burden.
Although he leads in front of the people,
    the people do not feel him as a threat.
Hence, the world supports him with no objection.
    This is because he does not contend,
    therefore, he is above all competition.

# 三寶章　第六十七

天下皆謂我道大，似不肖。夫唯大，故似不肖。
若肖，久矣其細也夫。我有三寶，持而保之。
一曰慈，二曰儉，三曰不敢爲天下先。
慈故能勇，儉故能廣，不敢爲天下先，故能成器長。
今舍慈且勇，舍儉且廣，舍後且先，死矣！
夫慈以戰則勝，以守則固。天將救之，以慈衛之。

# CHAPTER SIXTY-SEVEN

The whole world says the TAO that I have attained is so great that
    IT seems unreal.
Because IT is indeed so great, thus IT seemed unreal.
If IT were real, IT would have been insignificantly small.


I have THREE TREASURES that I hold and guard.
    The first is KINDNESS.
    The second is SIMPLICITY.
    The third is HUMBLENESS.
With KINDNESS, one can be courageous.
With SIMPLICITY, one can be generous.
With HUMBLENESS, one can be the lead to provide guidance.


Now, if one abandons kindness and yet tries to be courageous,
if one abandons simplicity and yet tries to be generous,
if one abandons humbleness and yet tries to lead as guidance,
    he is doomed to perish.


One who fights a battle with kindness shall win.
One who keeps guard with kindness shall secure.
Even the great nature shall save him and protect him with kindness.

## 不爭章　第六十八

善爲士者不武，
善戰者不怒，
善勝敵者不與，
善用人者爲之下。
是謂不爭之德，
是謂用人之力，
是謂配天古之極。

# CHAPTER SIXTY-EIGHT

A faithful TAO cultivator does not use force.

A good warrior does not lose his temper.

A great conqueror does not challenge others.

A good leader is humble.


This is called the virtue of peace with no contention.

This is also regarded as competence to make good use of the effort
of people.

Such is regarded as achieving harmony with nature.

Such is the perfect " Oneness" of true nature.

The greatest wisdom of Lao-Tze

TAO TE CHING

162

# 用兵章 第六十九

用兵有言：吾不敢爲主而爲客，不敢進寸而退尺。
是謂行無行，攘無臂，扔無敵，執無兵。
禍莫大於輕敵，輕敵幾喪吾寶。故抗兵相加，哀者勝矣。

## CHAPTER  SIXTY-NINE

In warfare, there is a saying of such strategy:

    I would rather take a defensive position than to make an initial
    offensive move.

    I would rather withdraw a foot than to march forward one inch.

Such is called to advance without advancement;

    To defeat without arm force;

    To fight as if there were no enemy;

    To carry weapons as if there were no weapons and thus
    no need for the use of weapons.

There is no greater disaster than to underestimate the enemy.

To do so may cost one to lose his valuable life.

Therefore, when two armies engage in a battle,

    the party that feels the sorrow of killing shall win.

道德經 TAO TE CHING

# 懷玉章 第七十

吾言甚易知，甚易行。天下莫能知，莫能行。

言有宗，事有君。

夫唯無知，是以不我知。

知我者希，則我者貴。是以聖人被褐懷玉。

## CHAPTER SEVENTY

My words of TAO is easy to understand and to practice.

However, the world can neither understand nor practice them.

In my words of TAO, there is the subtle truth.

In my deeds, there is the WAY of TAO.

Because people do not understand these,

therefore they do not understand me.

Those who know me are few.

Hence, the essence of TAO appears to be more honorable

and precious.

Thus, a saint may dress in ordinary coarse clothing,

yet has a heart of gem with the true essence within.

# 不病章 第七十一

知，不知，上；不知，知，病。
夫唯病病，是以不病。
聖人不病，以其病病，是以不病。

## CHAPTER SEVENTY-ONE

One who knows what people do not know,
　　is a person of enlightenment.

One who pretends to know what he is ignorant of, is at fault.

He who is aware of what he does not know, shall not be at fault.

Therefore, a saint is flawless for he is aware of what he truly knows
　　and what he knows not, hence he is flawless.

# 畏威章　第七十二

民不畏威，則大威至。無狎其所居，無厭其所生。
夫唯不厭，是以不厭。
是以聖人自知不自見，自愛不自貴。故去彼取此。

## CHAPTER　SEVENTY-TWO

When people do not respect the authority,
　　there shall be great misfortune.
Do not interfere with the people's livelihood.
Do not despise their living.
Because there is no detest against the people,
　　therefore the people do not detest against the authority.

The saint realizes his true nature and hence
　　does not distinguish himself.
He has a sense of self-respect and thus does not exalt himself.
Therefore, he rejects those that are self-distinguished and
　　self-exalted. And abides by these that are self-awareness and
　　self-respect.

# 天網章　第七十三

勇於敢則殺，勇於不敢則活。此兩者，或利或害，天之所惡，孰知
其故？是以聖人猶難之。天之道，不爭而善勝，不言而善應，不召
而自來，繟然而善謀。天網恢恢，疏而不失。

## CHAPTER SEVENTY--THREE

He who is brave in being daring, acts recklessly and shall be killed.
He who is brave but acts cautiously and kindly shall live.
Of these two, one is beneficial while the other is harmful.

What nature wishes, who may know what the reasons are?
Thus, the saint is aware of the subtlety and profoundness of the
    Nature's WAY, so he takes great caution in practicing IT.

The TAO of Nature,
    does not contend, yet easily wins.
    does not speak, yet always responds.
    does not summon, yet all things gather.
    does not contemplate as if at ease, yet all plans were devised
    perfectly.

The Law of Nature is like a giant web,
    although sparsely meshed, nothing can slip through.

The greatest wisdom of Lao-Tze

道德經
TAO TE CHING

# 司殺章 第七十四

民不畏死，奈何以死懼之！若使民常畏死，而爲奇者，吾得執而殺
之，孰敢？常有司殺者，殺。夫代司殺者，殺，是謂代大匠斲，夫
代大匠斲者：希有不傷其手矣。

## CHAPTER SEVENTY-FOUR

When people do not fear death,
　　there is no use trying to threaten them with death.
If people value their lives, and those who break the law were being
　　executed, then who would dare to commit criminal act?

The life and death of all beings are handled by the executioner
　　of Nature.
Those who substitute the nature executioner to kill,
　　is like replacing the master carpenter to chop the wood.
One who substitutes the master carpenter to chop the wood,
　　rarely does not hurt his hands.

## 貴生章 第七十五

民之饑，以其上食稅之多，是以饑。

民之難治，以其上之有爲，是以難治。

民之輕死，以其上求生之厚，是以輕死。

夫唯無以生爲者，是賢於貴生。

## CHAPTER SEVENTY-FIVE

People starved because the ruler taxed too heavily.

People are difficult to be ruled, because the ruler governs with
    personal desire and establishes too many laws to confuse
    the people.
    Therefore the people are difficult to be ruled.

People take death lightly, because the ruler pursues after
    luxurious life and depletes the people. Therefore the people
    take death lightly.

One who does not value his life with self-desire, truly cherishes his life.

# 柔弱章　第七十六

人之生也柔弱，其死也堅強。萬物草木之生也柔脆，其死也枯槁。
故堅強者，死之徒；柔弱者，生之徒。
是以兵強則不勝，木強則兵。強大處下，柔弱處上。

## CHAPTER SEVENTY-SIX

When a man is alive, he is soft and supple.

When he dies, the body becomes hard and stiff.

When a plant is alive, it is soft and flexible.

When it is dead, it becomes dry and brittle.

Therefore, hard and rigid shall lead to death.

    Soft and gentle shall lead to life.

Thus, a strong army with rigid force shall not win.

    A thick and big tree will be cut down for its use.

The big and strong will take an inferior position.

The soft and gentle will take a superior position.

# 天道章　第七十七

天之道，其猶張弓與！高者抑之，下者舉之；
有餘者損之，不足者補之。
天之道損有餘，而補不足；人之道則不然，損不足，以奉有餘。
孰能有餘以奉天下？唯有道者。
是以聖人，爲而不恃，功成而不處，其不欲見賢。

# CHAPTER SEVENTY-SEVEN

The TAO of Nature is like stretching a bow.
    When the stretch is too high, it needs to be pressed down.
    When the stretch is too low, it needs to be raised high.

The excess will be reduced.
The deficient will be replenished.

The TAO of Nature is to reduce the excessive and to replenish
    the  insufficient.
The TAO of man, however is otherwise.
    It takes from the needy to serve those who already have
    a surplus.

Who can spare one's surplus to serve the world?
    A person of TAO.
Thus, a saint acts without holding on to the achievements.
    He accomplishes but does not claim for credit.
    He has no desire to distinguish himself.

## 水德章　第七十八

天下莫柔弱於水，而攻堅強者莫之能勝。
以其無以易之。弱之勝強，柔之勝剛。
天下莫不知，莫能行。
是以聖人云：受國之垢，是謂社稷主；
受國不祥，是謂天下王。正言若反。

道德經　TAO TE CHING

# CHAPTER SEVENTY-EIGHT

There is nothing in this world that is softer and meeker than water.
Even those that can conquer the strong and hard,
    are still not superior than water.
Nothing can substitute it.

Hence, what is soft can overcome the strong.
    What is gentle can overcome the strength.
This is known by the world.
    However, people cannot put it into practice.

Therefore, the saint said as follow:
    He who can take the disgrace of a nation,
        is said to be the master of the nation.
    He who can bear the misfortune of a nation,
        is said to be the ruler of the world.

Truthful words may seem to be the reverse of worldly practices.

道德經

花開富貴情意濃
己卯一九九年正春梁溪屋王繼寬畫

# 左契章 第七十九

和大怨必有餘怨，安可以爲善？是以聖人執左契，而不責於人。
有德司契，無德司徹。天道無親，常與善人。

## CHAPTER    SEVENTY-NINE

When a great resentment has resulted,

    even if one tries to reconcile and make peace,

      there is bound to leave some remaining resentment.

Thus, how can this be considered as a good settlement?

Therefore, a saint cultivates himself with introspection and

    self-discipline without blaming others for faults.

This is like the ancient custom which acts by holding on to the

    left part of the tally as a debtor that demands nothing

    from others.

Hence, a person of virtue acts as if he were the debtor.

    And a person without virtue acts as if he were the

    creditor that demands only from others.

The TAO of Nature is impersonal which makes no exception

    to anyone.

IT always assists those that are kind and virtuous.

## 不徒章 第八十

小國寡民，使有什伯之器而不用，
使民重死而不遠徒。
雖有舟輿，無所乘之；
雖有甲兵，無所陳之。
使人復結繩而用之。
甘其食，美其服，安其居，樂其俗。
鄰國相望，雞犬之聲相聞，
民至老死不相往來。

# CHAPTER EIGHTY

An ideal nation is small and with few people.
Although there are abundant weapons, there is no need for the use.
Let the people cherish their life and not pursue after fame and wealth,
    so that they have no intention to move to faraway places.
Although there are boats and carriages, no one will ride them.
Although there are weapons and armors, there is no occasion to
    display them.

Let the people return to the ancient simple life where knotting
    ropes were used to record every event.
People would then enjoy the simple food, simple clothing,
    and be contented with a simple life.
And they shall live happily with the traditional customs.

Neighbors of the nations overlook one another in the near distance.
    The barks of dogs and crowing of cocks can be heard.
    Yet people are so contented that they enjoy their life
    without ever visiting each other.

# 不積章　第八十一

信言不美，美言不信。善者不辯，辯者不善。
知者不博，博者不知。
聖人不積。既以為人，己愈有，既以與人，己愈多。
天之道，利而不害；聖人之道，為而不爭。

## CHAPTER　EIGHTY-ONE

Words of truth are not pleasing.
Pleasing words are not truthful.

The wise one does not argue. He who argues is not wise.
A wise man of TAO knows the subtle truth,
    and may not be learned.
A learned person is knowledgeable but may not
    know the subtle truth of TAO.
A saint does not possess and accumulate surplus for
    personal desire.
    The more he helps others, the richer his life becomes.
    The more he gives to others, the more he gets in return.

The TAO of Nature benefits and does not harm.
The WAY of a saint is to act naturally without contention.

TAO TE CHING

# TAO TE CHING

*Truth About Oneself*

*Truth About Oneness*

TE: Towards Eternity
CHING : The WAY of Life

*TAO is the essence of the complete and absolute TRUTH that transcends all differences among the various religious teachings and practices.*

*TAO is the life, the beauty and the light that shines through all beings like a heart of gem that centers with the radiance of glory.*

道德經

*TAO is the heavenly eye that sees through all darkness, confusion, sorrow and pain.*

*Blessed are the ones:*

> *Who see with the sacred eye*
> *Who hear with the sacred eye*
> *Who speak with the sacred eye*
> *Who act with the sacred eye*

*TAO of the Millenium:*
> *Seek and thou shall receive*

國家圖書館出版品預行編目資料

道德經 = Tao Te Ching : the greatest
wisdom of Lao-Tze / 孫莉莉譯. -- 初版. -
- 臺北市 ： 基礎文教, 2001〔民90〕
面； 公分

中英對照
ISBN 957-9109-22-2（精裝）

1.道德經

121.31                                    90019593

# 道德經（*TAO TE CHING*）

譯　者　孫莉莉

出　版　基礎道德文化教育基金會

發行所　基礎道德文化教育基金會

　　　　地址 / 台北市 108 萬華區寶興街 188 巷 2 號

　　　　電話 / (02)23056278

　　　　傳真 / (02)23070408

　　　　www 網址：HTTP://www.1-kuan-tao.org.tw

　　　　E-mail:ikutao@ms47.hinet.net

　　　　　　ikutao@mail.1-kuan-tao.org.tw

　　　　編　號　FUNDATION 00020

　　　　行政院新聞局登記局版臺業字第 4898 號

初版一刷　西元 2002 年 1 月

定　　價　新台幣九九〇元（國外另加郵費）